WINTER SOUL

Poetic Truths in the Life of me

Adrianna Irizarry

ISBN - 10: 0988461765
ISBN – 13: 978-0-9884617-6-5

CONTENTS

All I Ask Of You

Amen

Darkness Reigns

Duty Unforgiving

Inner War

Lie to Me

Love Dream

Man for me

Only I Can Lead to Bliss

Sides of Mind

Soul of a Lost Girl

The Girl I Used To Be

True To Who I Am

Walk Away

Winter Soul

Always be Here

Brave Face

Desire

Future Love

Let This Die in Vain

Life is What it Cost

Love you, Love me

My Fears

Open Mind, Open Heart

Silent Love

Stormy Past

The Ride

Until Death Can Fully Reign

Wanton Pleasure

Without a Soul

Answer to my Pain

Burdened

Distant Light

Hope & Love vs. Hate

Liberty at a Cost

Life, Hope, and Love

Love's Fall

Nothing Less

Quiet Strength

Soon to be

Terrors of my Soul

The Way I Kept It

Use Me

Will

ACKNOWLEDGMENTS

Thank you to my editor at Worth Reading for formatting and editing this book for publication.
(www.WorthReading.weebly.com)
.

ALL I ASK OF YOU

You may not understand me,
   but I don't really care.
You try to bring me down,
   with your rumors, try to scare.

Let me tell you one thing –
You are not my life!
You are not important!
You are not worth the strife!

I live my life in happiness.
I live my life in pain.
I live the way I want to,
   in sun or in the rain

You may not understand it,
   but I don't ask you too.
Just let me live my life in peace.
That's all I ask of you.

ALWAYS BE HERE

When you trip and fall,
  are down and out.
When you change your mind,
  when you're full of doubt.

When you seem to change,
  so radically over night;
become someone new,
  the old you out of sight –

I'll be here.

When you fail at your dreams;
  lose out in love.
When you're at your worst;
  lost faith above.

If you're feeling hurt;
  full of anger and pain.
When you lash out at me.
When your souls in the rain –

I'll be here.

When you go for your passions.
If you freak out and quit.
When you forget you have allies.
If you fight or submit.

When others reject you;
  can't see who you are.
When you go through the seasons.
When we drift apart –

I'll be here.

I'm not some half-assed buddy;
  some disinterested pal.
I won't leave you alone;
I'll stay strong. I shall.

Despite what has happened;
  I will always be near.
I will be your shoulder;
  your listening ear.

So, pay attention my friend.
If you're angry or dear.
No matter what you are going through,
I will always be here.

ANSWER TO MY PAIN

Why do I love you,
  if you don't love me back?
Why do I give to others,
  when all they see is what I lack?

Why does one bother,
  with this day-to-day called life?
Where is the peace I want;
  why not love instead of strife?

Why do people choose to hurt?
Is loving so hard to do?
Why must you be cruel to me,
  when I've been kind to you?

Why do I continue on,
  no guard around my heart?
Why do I allow abuse,
  when I see a brand new start?

To answer all these questions;
  to sum up all my pain.
What I've lost is not important,
I treasure what I've gained.

The pain that you have caused me,
  I will not let it stay.
You cannot turn me into

another broken stray.

So regardless of your mocking,
  regardless of the pain;
I will have an open heart,
  my love will ever reign.

AMEN

Drowning, drowning,
  sinking to the ground.
Embracing worldly sin,
  by sin is how I'm bound.

Crying, hurting
  deep within.
I pray, eyes closed –
  "forgive my sin."

I know I'm weak.
I fight for strength.
I crawl through the dark,
  up jagged banks.

My emotions are
  my enemy.
I trust in you
  to set me free.

Again, I try
  to live my life,
  away from sin,
  out of strife.

Maybe this time
  I will succeed.
Stand by my side,
  you're all I need.

So regardless of your mocking,
  regardless of the pain;
I will have an open heart,
  my love will ever reign.

BRAVE FACE

How can anyone know my pain?
I keep it locked away.
The storms that war inside me,
  one day I know I'll pay.

I put on a brave face.
Everyone sees me smile.
They would be shocked beyond belief,
  if in my shoes they walked a mile.

I must be brave;
  stay strong and hard.
For if they see my weakness,
  then I would fall apart.

The pain that courses through me;
  the revulsion of my past,
No one would come near me,
  if I had let it last.

So day to day I fight it;
  try to wear a mask.
If I smile hard enough,
  perhaps hope will come to pass.

But no matter what today is,
I still have my past.

It will always haunt me;
Forever it will last.

BURDENED

A burden so great
  I cannot bear.
I scream and cry
  into the air

No one to hear.
No one around.
If I were to die,
  would I be found?

I struggle and fight,
  but can I win.
Each battle I face;
  each cursed sin.

I hide my pain
  down deep within.
Drown it out,
  with all my sin.

For just one moment,
  I wish to breathe;
  to forget my burdens,
  and to be free.

DARKNESS REIGNS

Can no one hear me cry!
In my heart, I feel such pain.
No matter how I try,
  I stand in never-ending rain

My dreams reel and dance,
  live before my eyes
I bow my head. There is no chance.
My dreams all pass and die.

Nothingness that binds me.
My Soul will ever pay.
No hope for love tomorrow.
For pain stole my yesterday.

The cold, the rain, surrounds me;
  wraps me in its state.
Hard to move, hard to breath;
  You can't escape your fate.

What is there to live for
  in a world that knows no shame.
No hope for love tomorrow,
  in darkness we'll remain.

DESIRE

I wonder where I'm going,
  for who can truly know.
I am racing with desire,
  and tossing to and fro.

My dreams are all around me;
  yet so very far away.
I'm dancing to the beat of fate;
  from fate I want to stray.

To make my own choices;
  fulfill some destiny.
Lord only knows where I am going,
  but I can't wait to see.

I will shine among the stars,
  and the world will know my name.
Changing the life before me;
  my dreams will never tame.

I must stay determined;
  not swayed by those who've failed.
A believer and a dreamer,
  I will blaze a brand new trail.

May my dreams shine ever bright;
  will and passion never dim.
Staying strong throughout the night,

for I believe that I can win.

DISTANT LIGHT

Searching in the darkness,
   I can see the light.
I stride with length to meet it;
   I struggle with the fight.

It stays far in the distance;
   never closer to me.
Still I strive to reach it,
   for with it I want to be.

Laboring in life,
   struggle day and night.
I will continue steadily;
   I will push with all my might.

One day I will reach it,
   though I know not what it is.
I will reach the light that's distant,
   before my own begins to dim.

DUTY UNFORGIVING

I stand alone in anger,
　glaring from my soul.
The men above me cowards,
　yet they sit upon the throne.

I am bound to them by duty,
　yet my own mind does rebel.
I must suffer all in silence,
　'You're wrong!' I cannot yell.

Forced to be less for them,
　I've swallowed so much pride.
Duty pushing down on me,
　until I suffocate and cry.

Unforgiving is my burden,
　heavy is my heart.
What is right and what we do,
　are often worlds apart.

FUTURE LOVE

I miss you through the seasons,
  though your name I do not know.
I think of how you'd love me,
  here close or far from home.

I tell myself be patient,
  you are somewhere in my life.
One day you'll say I love you,
  and we'll be man and wife.

So today, I'll stick to dreaming.
One day I'll see your face.
You'll look at me so knowingly,
  and everything will fall in place.

HOPE AND LOVE VS. HATE

Why people hate each other,
  then blame it on reality,
  is so silly and ridiculous,
  it is simply beyond me.

People say that the world is cruel,
  it's a dark and spiteful place;
  that kindness is a dream,
  it's the darkness you must face.

But I must disagree,
  with this benighted state of mind.
It's all about perspective,
  and I'll forever believe in mine.

Kindness is not a dream,
  trust isn't doomed to fail;
  hope is shared by all,
  love, not just a tale.

To all of those out there,
  who share this disbelief;
  who doubt in people's decency,
  you are easily deceived.

Hope and Love –

Two great powers known to man.
Although difficult to follow,
   don't be scared to take a stand.

Belief in love isn't ignorance,
   hate not the truth of life.
Although many cannot see it,
   we must not give up the fight.

And I will do my best,
   to live my life as such;
   full of generosity and love,
   how's the same of you too much?

INNER WAR

How many times must I say it;
  must I feel this through my soul?
Why must it rage throughout me,
  wild, without control?

The others do not see me,
  the things inside my mind.
They would not believe it,
  the dark the chains do bind.

I can feel it crawling in me,
  my soul exposed and pained.
On the brink of a disaster,
  pray for lights continued reign.

Tired of all the fighting,
  the demons, inner wars.
When will I be free of it,
  Feel this darkness nevermore?

LET THIS DIE IN VAIN

Drag me under water,
  I must learn to swim.
Drown me with your words,
  And let the games begin.

I know that you don't hate me,
  though it's hard to see your love.
You stab at me with hope,
  that guilt will drip with blood.

I try to satisfy your needs,
  though your fear is all too strong.
Because you're scared, you tear at me,
  ignoring what is wrong.

I cannot do it anymore,
  I am crawling on the ground.
My tears and pain, they drip from me,
  our blood is how I'm bound.

You've used me into nothingness,
  I'm numb from all the pain.
I've carried you for far too long,
  now let this die in vain.

LIBERTY AT A COST

Liberty from you.
Liberty for me.
No ill feelings.
Peace is all I seek.

The bonds are broken.
My emotions shattered.
I did it for me;
   although that doesn't matter.

Not to you,
   for in your mind,
I have betrayed;
   but you are blind.

I love you still,
I hope you know.
I always will,
   despite your show.

I sigh and breathe;
I thought I'd feel,
   much better than this.
So what's the deal?

Liberty seems
   to come at a cost.
I have freed myself,

but for a loss.

I love you still.
I hope you know,
  though free from you;
  this will ever be so.

LIE TO ME

Looking at you now,
  I see it's all gone wrong.
Looking at you now,
  I hear that sad, sad song.

I know the rains have come in,
  and the blue skies have gone away;
  but baby please lie to me,
  if just for one more day.

I thought that we had made it.
I thought we were so good.
But baby, I was oh so wrong.
  and I miss where I thought I stood.

I guess I should have seen it.
You never loved me as I did you.
I thought we were so happy.
All you were lacking was the truth.

So baby, please lie to me.
Just for one more day.
Help me not to feel the pain,
  of seeing you walk away.

LIFE IS WHAT IT COST

I can feel the life within me,
  draining far away;
The blood seeping from my soul,
  tears falling night and day.

Pain inside me welling,
  I have my eyes shut tight;
Sobbing, screaming, gasping,
  I reach for the sunlight.

Fire exploding from me,
  I have to run away.
Reaching for my happiness,
  for that far escape.

The rain pours down heavily,
  I sink down to the ground.
The wind rages all around me,
  the mud is where I'm found.

I see the fire dissipate,
  the hope I had is lost.
I sink deeper in this swamp,
  my life is what it cost.

LOVE, HOPE, AND DREAM

Everything seems clearer,
   the beauty more divine.
Life just seems much purer,
   as I walk a steady line.

Peace and love inside of me,
   for everything I see.
The joy is overwhelming,
   and I feel I've been set free.

My sight no longer hazy,
   confusion's out the door.
Anger's dissipating,
   and I'll love forever more.

I wish I could describe it,
   this great and natural high.
A sort of type euphoria,
   in every minute of my life.

Call it a positive outlook,
   an innocent state of mind.
But after all I've been through,
   I thought this I'd never find

So thank you to the heavens,
   to the man down here on earth;
   to the good souls I've encountered,

to my own soul's sense of worth.

This new life I have ahead of me,
  is a treasure I won't let go.
Life is out before me,
  and I know who loves me so.

LOVE DREAM

Gentle hands graze my back,
  as tender lips descend;
Barely touching, kissing, loving,
  I pray that this won't end.

No pressure and no judgment,
  my heart and soul secure.
In the arms of this gentle man,
  I feel wonderful and sure.

Forever seems so tangible,
  like we could never die.
Our love lasting through the years,
  how could it not survive.

His fingers stroke my hair now,
  he strokes it past my ear;
  his eyes are smiling at me,
  and they banish all my fears.

I now know what true love is,
  what I can't live without.
We will love like this forever,
  of this I have no doubt

LOVE YOU, LOVE ME

How can I say I'm sorry.
I am full of regret.
Not for my actions,
  but the tears that you have shed.

I know that I've caused them,
  but you've caused mine too.
We've been warring like soldiers,
  what else could we do?

You had your reasons,
  and I certainly had mine;
  but was it all worth it?
The pain full of pride?

I look back and wonder,
  how it all came to this;
  but know that I've realized,
  I'll tell you my wish.

The times we spend laughing,
  I want to go on.
The times we spent shouting,
  I want to be gone.

It's hard to forgive,
  when we both think we're right;
  but regardless of that,

let's give up this fight.

I love you my mother,
  of this you should know.
No matter our fighting,
  this will always be so.

I want your forgiveness,
  but for only your tears;
  I have struggled for freedom,
  all through these years.

Now that we're past this,
  our love is set free.
Know that I love you.
I love you, love me.

LOVE'S FALL

Where you're at
  is not your fate to be.
I know you're scared
  to be with me.

The things I said,
  may have crossed the line;
  but I'd say them again,
  for true love to find.

Where you're at
  is great for you.
To be with me,
  could fail, it's true.

I also know
  how great we are.
Just please trust me;
  and we will go far.

A leap of faith
  is all I ask.
To not regret
  when we look back.

Don't let the fear of guilt
  control your fate.
I'm standing here,

don't make me wait.

My hand is out,
  to you I call.
I'll hold you tight,
  don't fear love's fall.

MAN FOR ME

You look at me and smile.
I smile in return.
You look amazing in the moonlight.
One touch and fires burn.

You stroke my cheek so gently.
Your eyes so warm and kind.
Time has slowed to stopping.
I have no doubts in mind.

You pull me closer.
I can't help but blush.
Your strong arms encompass me.
It's such a wondrous rush.

My heart is beating faster.
Your fingers gently lift my chin.
I hold my breath and close my eyes,
  to mine your lips descend.

I breathe in deep with pleasure;
  with a smile, let out a sigh.
My dream is so inviting,
  I don't want to open my eyes.

I lay in bed alone.
This night, not like my dream.
Soon though it will pass,
  and I'll find a man for me.

MY FEARS

You are the greatest man
  I have ever met
You pull me close;
  do you see me yet?

My greatest fear
  is you will see
  who I truly am;
  deep inside of me.

How could you love
  someone like me?
My past mistakes;
  the sins that be?

You are the best,
  and I'm a mess.
How could you settle
  for me, for less?

I close my eyes
  and I pray strong,
  that your eyes stay closed,
  forever long.

NOTHING LESS

My desires are simple;
  to gain them, I've a plan –
To hold fast to my heart,
  for the true love of one man.

I've been plagued with sorrows;
  had pain shatter my heart.
Cried tears of humiliation,
  had my soul torn apart.

My past holds many demons,
  insecurities and pain.
I've fought to overcome them,
  through a never ending rain.

But I stand firm and hold fast;
  my past's not who I am.
I deserve more than loneliness,
  I desire hope from just one man.

To feel safe within his arms,
  not ridiculed by his voice.
For him to love who I am,
  to be with me is his choice.

I want for something good,
  full of love and happiness.
A man who's eyes see just me,
I will settle for nothing less.

ONLY I CAN LEAD TO BLISS

I think of him and wonder,
  Could we ever be?
Could we roll around like thunder,
  Strike like lightning?

I think of all the times we've talked.
Were there any signals that you made?
When you spoke, did I hear,
  What you really had to say?

I carefully recall your words,
  Listen to your tone of voice.
I want there to be something,
  I want me to be your choice

I don't know where to go from here,
  but if I had to choose;
  I'd rather we be just friends,
  than to forever lose.

Your friendship is important,
  but my heart is dreaming loud.
Should I fly among the clouds,
  Or keep my feet upon the ground?

I don't know if we could ever be,
  but I will tell you this;
  I will not play games with you,

I would rather swing and miss.

If you want me you will say,
  Faith I must have in this.
I can only be myself,
  only that will lead to bliss.

OPEN HEART, OPEN MIND

Look at me.
It's hard to see
  who I am,
  what I could be.

You judge eyes closed,
  mouth open wide;
  you speak not from truth,
  but from a narrow mind.

I have an open heart;
  an open mind.
I forgive, armor up;
I try to be kind.

Be as you are.
Limit your heart.
I will live free,
  for that's just the start.

QUIET STRENGTH

When I am kind,
  you think me meek.
When I seek peace,
  you think me weak.

My strength is hidden
  out of sight.
No need for show,
  I know my might.

You think you know me;
  what I've been through.
You see me lacking,
  your point of view.

Why waste my breath,
  when you are blind.
You do not see me,
  though I can shine.

I will not fight you;
  oppose your opinions,
  for I am strong enough,
  to live on, in spite of them.

SIDES OF MIND

The mind is such a deep abyss
  of feelings and confusion.
A swirling storm of thoughts and dreams,
  and interweaved illusions.

Uncertain are your feelings,
  and the facts a doubtful truth.
Mind and soul contrast each other,
  and assurance is aloof.

You fill your mind with facts from books,
  you learn from past mistakes;
  and yet you never fill
  that ever open space.

Your mind can be a mighty partner,
  or be your worst affair.
Working towards an awesome fate,
  or for your soul's despair.

An awesome marriage, barely balanced,
  so tender yet so strong.
Between your many sides of mind,
  united ever long.

SILENT LOVE

A silent love,
  for one man I know.
Whose eyes are bright,
  and looks just so.

Whose smile captures
  my heart and soul.
A silent love,
  for one man I know.

He doesn't know it;
  how I truly feel,
  about how I wish,
  my dreams were real.

I think about him;
  how there could be us.
Then I remember,
  It's a dream, because –

Because I don't tell him,
  I keep it all inside.
Could he ever see,
  the feelings that I hide?

A silent love,
  for one man I know.

Could he ever love me,
  I truly hope so.

SOON TO BE

Sitting here, alone I think –
  I want to be with you.
I want to hold you close to me;
  want to love you through and through.

I think of all the times we'd share,
  the laughter, love, and joy.
I smile softly at these thoughts,
  this could never cloy

I wrap myself within these thoughts,
  the love I wish to find.
I know that you are out there,
  and soon you will be mine.

Though, until the day we meet,
  I will sit here all alone.
Thoughts of memories soon to be,
  may the gift of love be shown.

SOUL OF A LOST GIRL

A girl that lost her way,
  her beating heart grows weak.
Inner demons war away,
  but others view her meek.

A colorless horizon,
  A sky so full of grey.
Doubt at every corner,
  'worthless' they all say.

Tired of screaming, her voice is gone;
  yet no one knows her pain.
Wilting away in a quiet room,
  chilled by a lonesome rain.

Always tense, never at peace;
  her soul's personal cage.
She holds the key to her own release,
  but fails to see it through the rage.

She grinds her teeth in anger;
  heart aches with self disdain.
Sadness wells within her,
  all happiness was plain.

She walks around,
  lost among us,
  looking for some love.

Last threads of hope,
    pray won't be lost,
    with faith in up above.

STORMY PAST

Open me up.
What do you see?
My blood, my muscles –
  a life to be?

If you look harder,
  can you see the pain?
The storms, the chaos;
  the thunder, the rain?

I am my own world;
  ever as diverse as we.
Ever adapting and changing,
  if you look, can you see?

The purity of winter.
The unblemished snow.
The honesty that lies there;
  now you look below.

Below to the swamps,
  of a dark and guilty past.
The icky feel of yesterday,
  how long will it last?

The storm bellows all around.
The leaves kicked by its might.
Like the swamps of my past,

the storm blocks out the light.

The rain falls through my present;
  the wind assaulting, like my guilt.
Bright lighting strikes at me;
  the thunder roaring at what's built.

I don't deserve what I've become;
  this shaky masquerade.
Yet I cling to it so tightly,
  all I have is what I made.

TERRORS OF MY SOUL

The feelings deep inside me,
  are nothing new to man.
Anger, pain, depression,
  and I hate who I am.

Growing deep inside me;
  I want to fight and scream.
Destroy the very nature,
  of goodness inside me.

I want to screw my neighbor,
  though his name I do not know.
I want to kill my spirit,
  'til love no longer flows.

Cause trouble with a stranger;
  destroy my best friends heart.
Tear out the good inside of me,
  until I fall apart.

Weeping on the cold hard ground,
  curled up so very tight.
All this pain I cause myself,
  won't be just for tonight.

Tomorrow is a new dawn,
  and the pain continues still.
I have to have control of it,

though I know I never will.

The darkness inside of me is winning,
  it scares me half to death;
  but should it kill my spirit,
  then there'd be nothing left.

I did not yearn for this.
I wanted love inside my life.
Will that ever come to pass?
Could I see past all my strife?

Pain and anger hold me tight;
  forever part of me.
Dark terrors of my soul –
  Will they ever set me free?

THE GIRL I USED TO BE

I used to wish,
  oh how I used to wish,
  that I would be smart in the ways of this world.
That I would know the dark secrets,
  and spin the red desires as if they were silk,
  and I the spinning wheel.

I dreamt of adventure, of being sassy and keen.
The men would fall over themselves in desperation of me.
I would be the woman that bewitched the beast.
The darkness, the passion would live inside me.

Now I look back.

I wish I could be apart
  of the innocence that used to be me.
No more searing passions,
  or burning flames of desire.

I simply now wish
  that my soul were not shredded
  from the misuse of dreams.

The only wish that I carry now,
  in the depths of my tattered soul,
  is to find purity of peace and innocence.

To reject the hot poker of sinful wanting,

and arise from my ashes like the Phoenix.
Wash away the tears that stain like blood,
  and with a mocking laughter beat the odds.

I seek to find that peace once more,
  though it is I who strayed by my own desiring will.
I follow the path back to light,
  though littered with temptation it may be.

Regardless of the degradation of my heart,
  through the pain that was as much my fault
  as it was the others.

I will find once more that girl I used to be,
  and hold to her tight for all eternity.

THE RIDE

We lock our eyes together,
  that's how it all began.
My heart skipped a beat,
  so began fate's master plan.

No words exchanged between us,
  for we speak silently.

You walk across the room,
  how I want you desperately.

Disappearing from the crowd,
  we find a quiet place.
The world outside vanishes,
  as I stare up at your face.

I feel your body on me,
  powerful and strong.
We start to move together,
  like an ancient passion song.

Your lips ignite me deep within;
  your hands give and demand.
Riding on a rush so high,
I never want to land.

Now I close around you,
  and you move expertly.

My nails dig in your shoulders,
  as you thrust inside of me.

Time is lost among us,
  the world does not exist.
We spin and fly together,
  lost in a passionate tryst.

For a moment, we are one.
Our souls and body collide.
We know not how long it'll last,
  we just enjoy the ride.

THE WAY I KEPT IT

As I lay here in my bed,
  I think of all we never said.
The times I saw your perfect face,
  and how I spoke without a trace;
  without a trace of the love I felt,
  how it's my heart that you make melt.
You never knew how I truly felt,
  and that's the way I kept it.

My fears kept my mouth shut tight,
  my love and mind in constant fights;
  wishing you would just show me,
  a hint of the way things could be.
Of our hands held tight together,
  and I would never doubt; however,
  we don't share all that we weather,
  but that's the way I kept it.

I look into your eyes, I see,
  a future that will never be;
  you love another, never me,
  and that's the way you kept it.

TRUE TO WHO I AM

Walking through the crowd,
  I can't see your face.
With everyone around,
  you're gone without a trace.

Everyone just crowds me,
  yet there is no one there.
Their bodies are an empty shell,
  they're completely unaware.

They morph to mediocrity,
  seek normalcy in life.
They march together, lonely,
  slowly dying by the knife.

I cut free and run away,
  to me they're brain dead sheep.
Wearing masks of society,
  for all of them I weep.

I stand out from all of you,
  for this I'm very proud.
There is only one of me,
  no others in this crowd.

And should tomorrow be my last,
  at dawn my life would end.
I will smile as I fade away,
  for I stayed true to who I am.

UNTIL DEATH CAN FULLY REIGN

When days are but a lifeless dream,
  your sorrows harsh and great.
When no one is around it seems,
  in death's surreal debate.

It's hard to stay awake,
  in this daze that we call life.
In the sins that we partake,
  reaping never ending strife.

Mind screaming, head reeling,
  ever sinking to the floor.
The nothingness I'm feeling,
  that I'll feel for evermore.

The dark hollows of my mind;
  tight nothing of my soul.
My emotions that will bind,
  until life will take its toll.

In this emptiness I'll wait;
  bound by inner pain.
Continue death's debate,
  until death can fully reign.

USE ME

Tired of being walked on,
  as the sun sets on my smile.
Giving never getting,
  my soul's been dragged for miles.

You have dug yourself real deep,
  and you are cared for there.
You would stab me in my sleep,
  you don't know what is fair.

My love for you withstanding,
  you use it like a net.
Fishing for advantage,
  you done using yet?

I sigh and stress about you;
  I know you can survive.
I want to leave this battle.
What would He say, up on high?

I struggle with your battle,
  though I know it's not my own.
When is it I will leave you,
  to sow seeds you've sown.

WALK AWAY

Blood dripping from my fingers;
  skin gone from their tips.
Clawing at the hopeful;
  breaking into bits.

My tears fall to the dirt;
  I hope to grow some good.
But again the tears just fall,
  as I knew they always would.

My pain is all to help you,
  by blood I hold you near.
You slash at me in anger,
  you claw at me in fear.

On the ground I lay tired,
  the dirt so harsh and cold.
You dangle from my heartache;
  your needs have made you bold.

I look at my surroundings;
  the dungeon of my life.
Where have you been keeping me;
  I thought love was good and bright.

So I stand up in my dungeon,
  though you try and drag me down.
I walk from all that's broken;
  I just hope I can be found.

WANTON PLEASURE

I want your hands upon me.
I dream of your blue eyes.
I close my lids and wonder;
  If I should ever try.

Should I make the first move?
Should I even dare?
You seem untouchable to me,
  I should proceed with care.

But that doesn't stop me dreaming,
  of you night and day.
I feel you hands upon me;
  It feels good this way.

Close my eyes, indulging.
This steamy fantasy.
My lips they part in wanting.
Your strong hands caress me.

I breath in deep and smile.
Do to me all things.
Draw from me a gasp or two,
  thrust and make me scream.

I bite my lip with pleasure;
  these thoughts inside my head.
Could it ever come to pass?
Fierce pleasure in your bed?

WILL

I do things that I shouldn't,
and I don't understand why.
Why I put forth the temptation;
choose to fall instead of fly.

I cross the lines that I put down;
and bend the rules I make.
I ignore my own advice;
I try to fix but I just break.

I've twisted all I want around;
my actions, lost and blind.
My heart can barely recognize,
my dreams of love to find.

And now I realize
that the moment's finally here.
Choose the damned or the weary?
Life and love instead fear?

All this time it's me I've fought;
blaming others all around.
But it's me I've overcome,
just before I hit the ground.

Cheer for me, my triumph.
Forget my past mistakes.
For now I fly among the stars.
For will is all it takes.

WINTER SOUL

The icy sheets lay on the grass;
  the winter wind so cold.
This bitter white dead nothingness;
  Its presence is so bold.

Through a window, picturesque,
  a painting shows its wonder.
But in the snow, outside so cold;
  the winter shows its thunder.

Misunderstood. Possibly.
For winter has no friends.
The birds fly south,
  the leaves fall off;
  indoors become the trend.

In pain and fury winter cries;
  snow falling to the ground.
Winds call out to passerby's,
  though no one sticks around.

So looking at this white cold land;
  why can no one see?
The barren soul of loneliness,
  that's hiding inside me.

WITHOUT A HOME

In a crowed of strangers;
I stand alone.
In a group of friends;
I have no home.

I look for you;
  yet I can't find
  what others have.
To call you mine.

Should I just be,
  and others none?
You might pick me
  as number one.

I bow my head,
  let out a sigh.
I turn away,
  and say goodbye.

I will not be
  your second choice.
Some lack of options;
  I have a voice.

I will hold out
  for that man of mine.
Who will see me first;

put me front in line.

But sadly right now,
  I am alone;
  and yet again,
  without a home.

ABOUT THE AUTHOR:
ADRIANNA IRIZARRY

I started writing poetry when I was eighteen. I had written other things before, but never poetry. Then one day, fiercely inspired, I typed out Winter Soul – my very first poem. I realized that I not only had a knack for writing poetry, but a passion for it as well. So, whenever I was filled with emotion – whether positive or negative – I would jot it down. Soon, I had pages and pages of poetry in which I derived much pride. It was never my intention to publish my work; after all, who reads poetry anymore? Certainly not me. I always considered poetry to be stuffy, confusing, and vague. My dream was, and still is, to publish a novel. Don't mistake my meaning. My heart swells with pride knowing that out there, somewhere, someone is reading these words, so I ask only this...The poetry within these pages is a rare glimpse into my soul; the words an expression of my innermost emotions – so please be gentle.

www.ingramcontent.com/pod-product-compliance
Lightning Source LLC
LaVergne TN
LVHW051200080426
835508LV00021B/2729